CAMAS PUBLIC LIBRARY
CAMAS, WA

3 3277 00247 3499

D0538307

Landmark
Events in
American
History

# The Battle of the
# Little Bighorn

Michael V. Uschan

WORLD ALMANAC® LIBRARY

*With all my love to James and John Mike Bloedel – M.V.U.*

**Please visit our web site at:  www.worldalmanaclibrary.com**
For a free color catalog describing World Almanac® Library's list of high-quality books and multimedia programs, call 1-800-848-2928 (USA) or 1-800-387-3178 (Canada).  World Almanac® Library's fax:  (414) 332-3567.

**Library of Congress Cataloging-in-Publication Data**

Uschan, Michael V., 1948-
       The Battle of the Little Bighorn / by Michael V. Uschan.
          p. cm. — (Landmark events in American history)
       Summary:  Describes the causes, events, and aftermath of the fateful encounter at the Little Bighorn River on June 25, 1876, between the Seventh Cavalry troops commanded by Lieutenant Colonel Custer and the Cheyenne and Lakota Sioux led by Chiefs Sitting Bull and Crazy Horse.
       Includes bibliographical references and index.
       ISBN 0-8368-5338-5 (lib. bdg.)
       ISBN 0-8368-5352-0 (softcover)
       1.  Little Bighorn, Battle of the, Mont., 1876—Juvenile literature.  [1.  Little Bighorn, Battle of the, Mont., 1876.  2.  Custer, George Armstrong, 1839-1876.  3.  Indians of North America—Great Plains—Wars.]  I.  Title.  II.  Series.
       E83.876.U785   2002
       973.8'2—dc21                                                                    2002024632

This North American edition first published in 2002 by
**World Almanac® Library**
330 West Olive Street, Suite 100
Milwaukee, WI  53212  USA

This U.S. edition © 2002 by World Almanac® Library.

Produced by Discovery Books
Editor: Sabrina Crewe
Designer and page production: Sabine Beaupré
Photo researcher: Sabrina Crewe
Maps and diagrams: Stefan Chabluk
World Almanac® Library editorial direction: Mark J. Sachner
World Almanac® Library art direction: Tammy Gruenewald
World Almanac® Library production: Susan Ashley

Photo credits: Buffalo Bill Historical Center: pp. 5, 34; Corbis: cover, pp. 8, 11, 22, 23, 36, 43; Granger Collection: pp. 14, 15, 20–21, 28, 33, 39; Library of Congress: p. 41; National Park Service, Little Bighorn Battlefield National Monument: pp. 16, 18, 27, 29, 31, 35, 37, 38, 40; Nebraska State Historical Society: p. 7; North Wind Picture Archives: pp. 4, 9, 10, 12, 13, 24, 26, 42; Rushmore Photo and Gift: p. 17; West Point Military Academy Museum: p. 32.

All rights reserved.  No part of this book may be reproduced, stored in a retrieval system, or transmitted in any form or by any means, electronic, mechanical, photocopying, recording, or otherwise, without the prior written permission of the copyright holder.

Printed in the United States of America

1 2 3 4 5 6 7 8 9 06 05 04 03 02

# Contents

# Introduction

The Battle of the Little Bighorn took place in the summer of 1876 when the United States was celebrating its centennial, or first hundred years of independence. The population was growing, and the frontier was quickly moving westward.

## Victory on the Plains

On the hot, sunny afternoon of June 25, 1876, some 2,000 Plains Indian warriors swept down on 210 U.S. soldiers. The warriors were led by Sioux chiefs Sitting Bull and Crazy Horse, and the U.S. Army was commanded by Lieutenant Colonel George Armstrong Custer. In two short hours, the Native force killed all the U.S. soldiers.

## A Long War

This was a part of the battle that later became known as the Battle of the Little Bighorn. The battle was not the greatest military victory for Native Americans. It is, however, the most famous single encounter in the long war between whites and Native Americans in North America. For the Sioux and their allies, the victory at the Little Bighorn was only a prelude to final defeat. Within a few years, those who fought would be conquered and confined to **reservations**.

The Battle of the Little Bighorn is also known by two other names. These reflect the different perspectives that the two sides brought to the legendary confrontation.

## Greasy Grass

Descendants of Native Americans who fought remember it as the Battle of the Greasy Grass. "Greasy Grass," in Sioux, is the name of the valley of the Little Bighorn River in Montana where the two sides clashed. "Greasy grass" is also the rich, thick prairie grass that fed the horses of the Plains people and the buffalo they hunted. These animals were vital to the Plains Indians' **nomadic** way of life. It was a way of life that was being eroded as the United States violated every **treaty** it had made with the Plains people and broke every promise regarding Native lands.

## "Custer's Last Stand"

The fight in which Custer and his men were overcome is known as Custer's Last Stand. Custer was a heroic figure to white Americans even before his death. He had been a dashing young **cavalry** officer who caught his country's attention during the Civil War with his bravery in battle. This military hero's defeat and death became a symbol to many Americans. It made them more determined than ever to end Native resistance to white control. After the battle, the United States government intensified its war against Native people.

This type of picture is known as a pictograph. Painted on a deerskin by an unknown Sioux, it shows the Battle of the Little Bighorn.

# Chapter 1

# The Plains People

## People of the Plains

The Plains Indians who fought in the Battle of the Little Bighorn were descendants of Native people who had migrated across a vast, uninhabited continent thousands of years before. By 1590, when English people began arriving in what they called the "New World," it is estimated that several million Native Americans lived in what would one day become the United States.

The different tribes established their own cultures, traditions, and languages as they settled in the mountains, deserts, valleys, and prairies of North America. One of the most distinctive groups of Native people were those who settled on the Great Plains.

## The Sioux

The Indians of the Great Plains included the Arapaho, Cheyenne, Comanche, Crow, Iowa, Pawnee, and—strongest of all—the Sioux. Their name is taken from the word *nadouessioux*, meaning "treacherous snake," a term originally applied to the Sioux by the Ojibwa people and later used by whites. There were three main divisions of the Sioux **nation**: the Santee, the Teton, and the Yankton. They called themselves, respectively, the Dakota, Nakota, and Lakota.

The Great Plains extends westward from the Mississippi River to the Rocky Mountains and runs north and south between the present-day borders of neighboring Canada and Mexico. Like the rest of North America, the region was inhabited by Native people for thousands of years before white settlement. This map shows the homelands of the Native people of North America.

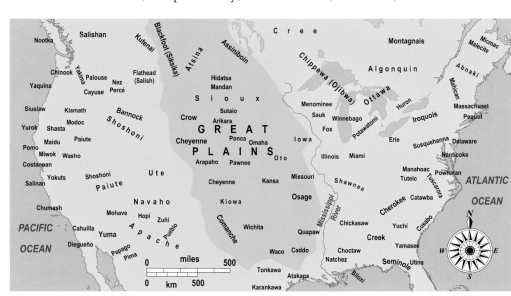

This tepee village of the Cheyenne people was photographed in 1880 near Fort Laramie in Wyoming. The Cheyenne people of the western Plains had allied themselves with the Sioux against the U.S. Army at Little Bighorn four years earlier.

The Sioux who lived in the western Plains and fought at the Little Bighorn were the Lakota. This branch of the Sioux was further divided into seven groups: the Blackfoot, Brulé, Hunkpapa, Miniconjou, Oglala, Sans Arcs, and Two-Kettle.

Plains Indians hunted antelope, deer, and elk, but the American bison—or buffalo—was their primary game and was vital to their survival. People on the Plains lived nomadic lives so they could follow buffalo herds, which roamed across a vast area. Buffalo meat was the main source of food for the Sioux. They used buffalo hides to make clothing and tepees. The Sioux used other parts of the buffalo in many ways, such as carving bones to make sewing needles.

## Indians or Native Americans?

Native Americans are called Indians because Christopher Columbus made a mistake. In 1492, when the Italian explorer sailed from Europe to the Caribbean, he thought he had reached a part of Asia. Europeans then referred to Asia as "the Indies," and Columbus named the people he met "Indians." The name came to be used for the original inhabitants of any area in the Americas. Although Indian became the common European-American term for Native Americans—and is still used by Natives and non-Natives alike—each nation or tribe has its own name. Many of these names translate simply as "The People."

### Horses and Guns

The life of the Plains Indians changed dramatically in the seventeenth century when horses were introduced to the Great Plains. Within a few decades, most Native groups had their own large herds. Horses made it easier for them to follow the buffalo herds that wandered the Great Plains in search of grass to eat and to kill the big, shaggy beasts. It had been very difficult to hunt buffalo on foot, but now hunters could gallop alongside the herds and kill many buffalo with bows and arrows or lances.

In the eighteenth century, Spanish, French, and English explorers and settlers again transformed Native life on the Plains by introducing a powerful new weapon: the gun. These firearms were single-shot

## Tepees and Travois

A Blackfoot Sioux family travels across the northern Plains with small children and household goods in travois.

As nomadic people, the Plains Indians needed dwellings they could quickly dismantle and transport to new locations. Their answer to this was the tepee, a cone-shaped tent made from buffalo hide. The hides were stretched over long poles and fastened to the ground with wooden pegs. The tepees had openings at the top to release smoke from fires people made to keep warm and to cook food over. They kept their tepees cool in summer by raising the sides to allow air to flow through and warm in winter by hanging heavy inner linings to keep out the cold.

The long poles that supported the tepees served another important purpose. When the group had to travel, the poles were tied into a V-shaped frame. Hides were then stretched over the poles, and the poles were fastened to a horse to make a travois. This device was dragged along the ground like a sled. Families loaded their household belongings onto the travois, and a horse pulled it to the next camp.

Plains warriors developed rituals to distinguish bravery in battle, including that of "counting coup." This was done by touching a fallen enemy, as shown here, or touching an opponent in battle without killing him.

**muzzle-loaders** that made it even easier to hunt buffalo. Like their European-American counterparts, Plains Indians also used them in warring against their enemies.

## A War Culture

The people of the Great Plains were fierce warriors, and war was a way of life for them. Warriors who could fight well and were brave in battle were honored above other tribal members. The Plains Indians did form alliances with other tribes, but generally any outsider was considered a potential enemy. Different groups battled for hunting grounds and raided each other to steal horses, the people's most valuable asset.

It was in one such conflict that the Sioux themselves were forced to move further west. The Sioux once lived along the Mississippi River in present-day Minnesota. But around 1700, the Ojibwa extended their territory by conquering the Sioux and driving them west. The Sioux ended up beyond the Missouri River in the area that is now South and North Dakota. This territory was already home to another group of people, the Crow. The Sioux defeated them and became their bitter enemies.

A group of settlers camps on the Plains during the 1850s on the way to California. Several trails to the West crossed Native lands, and travelers were frequently helped by Plains people who acted as guides, traded horses, and supplied food.

### "Barbarous" Habits

"Our civilization ought to take the place of their barbarous habits. We claim the right to control the soil they occupy, and we assume that it is our duty to coerce them, if necessary, into the adoption and practice of our habits and customs."

*Secretary of the Interior Columbus Delano, 1872*

## The White Man Comes

After the Louisiana Purchase of 1803 enlarged U.S. territory, white settlers living in America's original thirteen colonies began to venture westward in search of more land. In the mid-1800s, however, almost all of the soldiers, settlers, and **trappers** who ventured across the Great Plains were heading farther west to California and Oregon. There were scattered fights between them and Plains people but no major wars because the whites were not trying to settle there.

Conflict over the homelands of the Sioux and other Plains people was inevitable, however, because of

**Manifest** Destiny. This term was coined in 1845 by magazine editor John L. O'Sullivan. Writing in the *United States Magazine and Democratic Review*, he declared it was America's "manifest destiny to overspread the continent allotted by Providence for the free development of our yearly multiplying millions." The phrase came to symbolize the idea that white Americans should be able to extend the borders of their young nation all the way from the Atlantic Ocean to the Pacific Ocean.

At the heart of the Manifest Destiny philosophy was the belief that U.S. settlers had the right to take land away from Native Americans because white people's way of life was superior. Many white Americans believed that it was important for Indians to live like them. They thought Indians must adopt the Christian religion, learn to read and write, and become farmers instead of hunters, even if whites had to conquer them first and force them to do this. The great American dream of Manifest Destiny would lead to war with many peoples of the Plains.

Arapaho men sit in front of a rack drying buffalo meat at their camp in Kansas in 1870. The traditional culture of Plains people was one that many white settlers attempted to eradicate.

# Broken Promises

## Westward Bound

The end of the Civil War in 1865 unleashed a new wave of **emigrants** heading west, among them hundreds of miners intent on striking it rich by finding gold in Montana. Unfortunately for the Sioux, the best route to the gold fields—the Bozeman Trail—went through their territory. When the U.S. government began to build a new road to make travel easier, the Sioux rose up to protect their homeland. The Sioux were angry because the road crossed the Powder, Tongue, and Bighorn Rivers, slicing through the area where buffalo herds ranged. They also resented the three forts built by the U.S. Army to protect travelers.

## Red Cloud and William Fetterman

There had been sporadic fighting and minor uprisings by Plains tribes for several years. None was like the all-out war that started in 1866 and was led by Chief Red Cloud, an Oglala Sioux. Red Cloud was an intelligent military strategist. One of his battle plans resulted in what became known as the Fetterman Massacre.

William Fetterman was a young **infantry** captain at Fort Phil Kearny in Montana who once boasted arrogantly, "Give me a single

This army post, Fort Abraham Lincoln, is near Mandan, South Dakota, in the Sioux homelands. It was the base of the Seventh Cavalry, commanded by Lt. Col. Custer. Custer's house can be seen in front of the barracks.

company of **regulars** and I can whip a thousand Indians. With eighty men I could ride through the Sioux nation." On December 21, 1866, Red Cloud lured Fetterman's command of eighty men out of the protection of the fort and into an ambush. Fetterman and his entire unit were killed.

Red Cloud's victory over Fetterman vaulted the Oglala chief into a position of leadership among the Sioux as a whole, and the conflict soon became known as Red Cloud's War. The Sioux and their Cheyenne allies fought strongly for two more years.

## Red Cloud's Defeat

On August 2, 1868, Red Cloud led a thousand warriors in an attack on soldiers who had left the safety of Fort Kearny. The attack was eerily similar to the assault against Captain Fetterman, but this time the Sioux chief suffered a bitter defeat. The thirty-six men led by Captain James Powell had prepared for such an ambush by arming themselves with new **breech-loading** rifles that could fire bullets faster than old muzzle-loaders. Powell also brought wagons that had iron bottoms, and his soldiers used them to make a shield that protected them from bullets.

In the battle, Powell's men killed half of Red Cloud's men, shooting down wave after wave of mounted warriors. Years afterward, Red Cloud still mourned the deaths of so many of his warriors in that battle: "I lost them. They never fought again."

Chief Red Cloud of the Oglala Sioux was one of the few Native leaders to win concessions from the United States government. But the agreements giving the Sioux rights to their homelands were soon broken.

13

# Massacres

Both white Americans and Native people were guilty of brutal acts known as massacres, or mass killings. The Sand Creek Massacre in Colorado on November 29, 1864, is an example. At dawn that day, a force of 700 soldiers led by Colonel John Chivington attacked a sleeping Cheyenne village. Chivington believed some of its warriors had killed white settlers, even though the group, led by Chief Black Kettle, was known to be peaceful. Chivington ordered his troops to "Kill and scalp all [Native people] big and little." In the attack, 28 men and 105 women and children died.

Lieutenant Colonel Custer was involved in a similar incident (shown above) on the Washita River in Oklahoma. At dawn on November 27, 1868, Custer and his men charged a sleeping village believed to hold Cheyenne warriors who had killed settlers. Some historians refer to the Battle of the Washita as a massacre because so many women and children were killed—only 11 of the 103 who died were warriors. The unfortunate Black Kettle, still at peace with whites, was again present. He and his wife were killed.

## The Treaty of Fort Laramie

There were many battles and many deaths before the two sides finally agreed to peace terms in November 1868 in the Treaty of Fort Laramie. The treaty was unusually favorable to the Sioux. **Federal** officials, anxious to stop the fighting, gave in to Red Cloud's demands to abandon the new road and the army forts, including Fort Phil Kearny. Plains people burned the forts when the soldiers left.

An earlier agreement of 1851 had established a Sioux reservation that covered parts of what are now Wyoming, North Dakota, South Dakota, and Nebraska. The Treaty of Fort Laramie reduced the size of the Great Sioux Reservation to just the South Dakota area. The treaty also promised the Sioux they could keep their traditional home in the *Paha Sapa*, or Black Hills. This wooded, hilly region extended beyond the reservation land into Wyoming. The Sioux considered this area sacred. The Black Hills region was termed "**unceded** territory" by the United States government and would belong to the Plains people.

**One Promise Kept**
"They made us many promises, more than I can remember, but they never kept but one. They promised to take our land, and they took it."

*Red Cloud*

Negotiations between the Sioux and the U.S. government take place in a tent at Fort Laramie in 1868.

15

The treaty also granted the Native people rights to continue hunting in the unceded territory further west, in the Powder River country of Wyoming and Montana. These traditional buffalo hunting grounds included the Little Bighorn Valley. People who remained on the reservation and accepted food rations from government Indian agencies were called "agency Indians" and thought of as friendly. The Sioux who continued to roam and hunt beyond the reservation boundaries were considered "hostiles." In fact, many Sioux were neither one nor the other. They stayed on the reservation in the winter and roamed in the summer.

Red Cloud's victory would prove to be a hollow one. The treaty promised the Sioux the land "for as long as the grass shall grow." Within a few years, however, it would be taken away from them.

## Custer's Expedition

In 1874, a fact-finding expedition led by Lieutenant Colonel Custer helped determine the fate of the area. George Armstrong Custer had taken command of the Seventh Cavalry Regiment of the United

Custer's expedition of 1874 winds its way across the Plains. In a dispatch to the U.S. war department, Custer wrote that the expedition had found gold: "On some of the watercourses almost every panful of earth produced gold in small, but paying, quantities. The miners report that they found gold among the roots of the grass."

States Army in 1866 and had the reputation of being the army's most dashing "Indian fighter" and a brave if reckless soldier.

From July 2 to August 30, 1874, Custer led an expedition of twelve hundred men through the Black Hills. Custer was looking for a site for a new military post. For years, however, there had been rumors of gold in the Black Hills, and Custer was ordered to do some scientific exploration on the expedition. Sure enough, his scientists found traces of gold.

The area was off-limits to whites as part of the reservation and as unceded territory. But that did not stop gold **prospectors** from flocking there in great numbers. Towns such as Deadwood and Custer in Dakota Territory soon sprang up, and white settlers began to outnumber the Sioux in the Black Hills. By early 1876, the town of Custer alone had eleven thousand residents.

When Custer's report was made public, newspaper headlines boldly declared there was "GOLD!" in the Black Hills. Gold prospectors poured into the area. Deadwood, seen here in 1876, was one of the boom towns that soon appeared.

A gold-mining scene in the 1870s. To the poor men who became gold prospectors, the Black Hills held the hope of riches and a better life.

One reason whites and Native Americans fought so often was that they did not understand each other. Their cultures were different in many ways, especially in how they viewed land they warred over. Historian James West Davidson explains this culture clash: "What most separated white and Indian cultures were attitudes toward the land and all that was on it. Man, for the Indians, was a single part of a complex web of animals, plants, and other natural elements—all with souls of their own. Where Europeans viewed nature as a resource to be exploited, the Indians saw it as sacred."

This means that when whites looked at the Black Hills, they often saw gold, rich farm land, and other **natural resources** that could bring them wealth. They were also accustomed to the concept of private land ownership and the buying and selling of parcels of land. But to the Sioux, the land was a magnificent, wild country that could never be owned by any individual. The Paha Sapa were also sacred to them in a religious sense. They symbolized Wakan Tanka, meaning "great spirit," which was at the core of their spiritual life.

## Broken Treaty

Between 1874 and 1876, the Fort Laramie Treaty was continually violated as prospectors continued to invade the Black Hills. Many Sioux left the reservation to return to their old way of life. The Hunkpapa Sioux leader Sitting Bull pleaded, "Let us alone. Let us alone. We want only to be left alone." The Sioux also fought back, killing prospectors and raiding settlements. The U.S. government tried to buy the Black Hills to avoid further warfare, but the Sioux refused to sell the territory.

In December 1875, President Ulysses S. Grant signed an order requiring all Indians in the unceded territory to report to the reservation by January 31, 1876, or be considered hostiles. Grant's order broke the Fort Laramie Treaty, which had granted the Sioux the unceded land forever, and took away the Sioux's right to the land.

Even if the Plains people had wanted to obey the order, many never knew of it or did not have time to comply with it. As a result, thousands of people were declared hostile. In early 1876, General Philip Sheridan, who commanded U.S. forces in the West, began planning how to round up the Indians and force them onto the reservation. His plan would lead to the Battle of the Little Bighorn.

This map shows the Bozeman Trail that cut right through sacred hunting grounds of the Sioux. It also shows how successive treaties with the U.S. government reduced Sioux lands. Broken treaties reduced them even more.

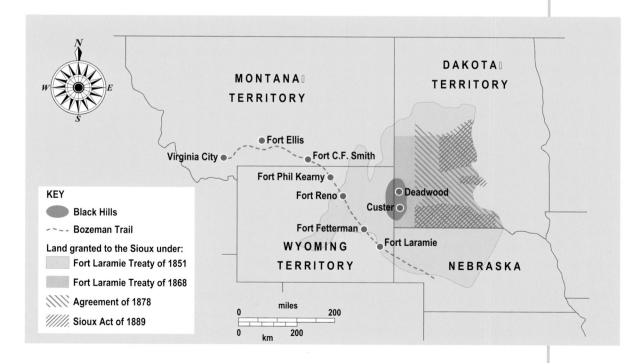

# The Army Moves in

The year 1876 marked the hundredth anniversary of the birth of the United States. In the preceding century, white and African Americans had grown in numbers from 3 million to about 44 million and surged westward to the Pacific Ocean. In that same period, the Native American population fell from 1 million to an estimated 300,000. Native people died in battle with whites. Even more, their communities were ravaged by diseases like smallpox and cholera that had been brought by settlers from Europe.

## A Vanishing Way of Life

By 1876, most Native groups had been defeated and forced onto reservations. Almost the only area in America still freely inhabited by its original inhabitants was the western Great Plains. But the traditional way of life was fast vanishing even there. The slaying of millions of buffalo in the 1870s by white hunters denied the Plains Indians their most important resource.

In 1889, Albert Bierstadt, one the West's greatest artists, painted a buffalo hunt to record a vanishing way of life. Only a few years before, this type of hunting had been a way of life for the Plains people.

Buffalo were hunted unmercifully by frontiersmen like William F. Cody, who earned the nickname "Buffalo Bill" by killing more than 4,200 in just eighteen months. From 1872 to 1874, nearly 3 million buffalo were killed each year. In 1860, there had been as many as 60 million buffalo. Within a decade, the giant herds had dwindled to only 13 million. In the first few years of the 1870s, millions more buffalo were slaughtered for their hides. The Plains became littered with buffalo bones while people went hungry.

## Plains People Gather

In that centennial year of the nation's birth, however, the Hunkpapa Sioux chief Sitting Bull was responsible for one last celebration of traditional life. Sitting Bull was respected by the Sioux not only as a warrior but as a spiritual

### Killing the Buffalo

"I can remember when the bison were so many that they could not be counted. But more and more [whites] came to kill them until they were only heaps of bones scattered where they used to be. The [whites] did not kill them to eat; they killed them for the metal that makes them crazy [gold, which they obtained by selling the hides]. You can see that the men who did this were crazy. They just killed and killed because they liked to do that. When we hunted bison, we killed only what we needed."

*Sioux leader Black Elk*

leader. In February, angry over the order confining his people to the Great Sioux Reservation, he invited Plains Indians to join him at Rosebud Creek in Montana Territory. He wanted Native people to band together to fight the whites and return to the traditional life they had once led, including hunting buffalo. The area near where Sitting Bull camped held the West's last big buffalo herd.

Through the spring of 1876, groups of Sioux, Cheyenne, and Arapaho flocked to Sitting Bull. By late June, several thousand men, women, and children had gathered to dance, feast, and revel in having regained their freedom to live the way they wanted. It was probably the largest gathering ever of Plains people. But the U.S. Army was already on its way to send them back to the reservations.

## Sitting Bull (c. 1831—1890)

Sitting Bull, or Tatanka Iyotake, was a Hunkpapa Sioux known for his distrust of white men and his determination to resist being dominated by them. By 1866, he was the principal chief of the Sioux because he was respected for his courage and wisdom. In his final years, Sitting Bull had to live on a reservation, a way of life he hated. When he was younger, he had criticized the Sioux who were living on reservations: "The whites may get me at last, as you say, but I will have good times till then. You are fools to make your-selves slaves to a piece of bacon, some **hardtack** and a little sugar and coffee."

This photograph was taken during the Civil War between 1861 and 1865. General Philip Sheridan, who commanded all U.S. forces in the West, stands on the left. On the right stands General George Crook, one of the three leaders in Sheridan's plan to round up the Plains Indians. Custer sits on the far right.

## Rounding Up Hostiles

General Philip Sheridan, then in charge of Western army forces, is notorious for having once claimed, "The only good Indian is a dead Indian." When some Sioux failed to return to the reservation in January, he drew up a plan to force them to comply with the order. The plan involved the use of three **columns** totaling more than 2,500 soldiers.

Sheridan ordered General George Crook to travel north from Fort Fetterman in Wyoming with about 1,200 men. General Alfred Terry, with Custer as one of his top officers, was to proceed west from Fort Abraham Lincoln in Dakota Territory with 1,300 soldiers. Colonel John Gibbon, with a force of 450, was to advance east from Fort Ellis in Montana. All three columns included cavalry and infantry units. The plan was to have them meet up and attack from all sides once the Native camp was located.

**Fierce Fighting
at the Rosebud**

"Indians were charging
boldly and rapidly
through the soldiers,
knocking them from their
horses with lances and
knives, dismounting and
killing them, cutting off
the arms of some in the
middle of the fight [as
trophies of war] and
carrying them away."

*Colonel Anson Miles describing the Battle of the Rosebud,
June 17, 1876*

## Battle of the Rosebud

Sheridan's master plan, however, never materialized. On June 17, the Oglala war chief Crazy Horse and a thousand of his warriors attacked Crook as he headed toward Rosebud Valley. The surprise attack was fierce and bloody. The Battle of the Rosebud raged for six hours, with the Sioux finally departing after killing twenty-eight soldiers and wounding fifty-six. One soldier reported, "They were on every hilltop, far and near. I had been in several Indian battles but never saw so many Indians at one time before . . . or [fight] so brave."

Crook was so shaken by the attack of a force much larger than he had expected to encounter that he retreated. Thus he was unable to help Custer at the Little Bighorn, which was only about 20 miles (32 kilometers) away. It was there where the three units were to have met to launch a united attack against the Native Americans.

General Crook's army moved out of Fort Fetterman and headed north toward the unceded territories in Montana. This engraving shows the column at Goose Creek on the day before the Battle of the Rosebud.

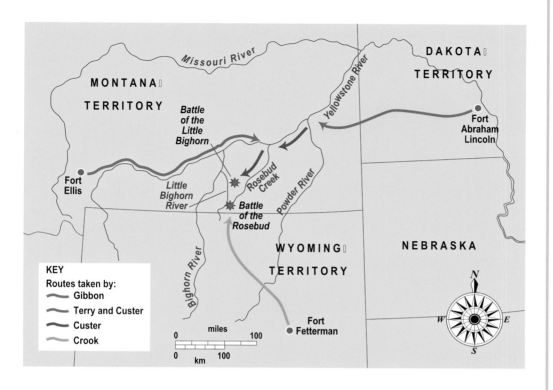

KEY
Routes taken by:
Gibbon
Terry and Custer
Custer
Crook

Gibbon and Terry's columns met at the junction of the Yellowstone River and Rosebud Creek, according to Sheridan's plan. Crook's men, however, had been attacked a few days before in the Battle of the Rosebud.

## Custer Sets Out

While a band cheerfully played "The Girl I Left Behind Me," a marching tune, the Seventh Cavalry had left Fort Abraham Lincoln on May 17. Custer's men made their way to the junction of the Yellowstone River and Rosebud Creek, where they were met by Gibbon's force. Both Custer and Gibbon received supplies there from the *Far West*, a steamboat that had arrived there.

On June 21, Terry met aboard the *Far West* with Gibbon and Custer to plan how to find and subdue the Plains Indians. It was believed they had moved from Rosebud Creek to the Little Bighorn River, and Terry's main worry was that they would flee when they sighted his soldiers.

Terry ordered Custer to head south down the Rosebud and then sweep west to the Little Bighorn while he and Gibbon would proceed west along the Yellowstone and then south to the Little Bighorn. Terry had still not heard from the defeated Crook, but he expected him to arrive shortly from the south to help trap the Native people. Although Terry's orders were flexible, he expected to meet up with Custer at the Little Bighorn on June 26.

## Getting Into Position

On June 22 at noon, Custer set out with a force of more than 600 men: 31 officers, 566 enlisted men, and about 35 Native **scouts**. Most of the scouts were Crows happy to fight their ancient enemy, the Sioux, but there were also four Sioux. Gibbon called out jokingly, "Now, Custer, don't be greedy, but wait for us." Custer replied cheerfully, "No, I will not."

Custer wanted to be the first to find the Native Americans, partly because he wanted the glory of a victory over them. He pushed his men hard, driving them 115 miles (185 km) from June 23

## Sitting Bull's Vision

A buffalo skull used as a sacred object of focus in the Sun Dance.

During their march in June 1876, Custer's men came upon Sitting Bull's vacated camp on the Rosebud. It was at this spot a couple of weeks before that Sitting Bull led his people in a Sun Dance. During this ceremony, dancers fasted and stared at a sacred object for days to bring on a vision. Sitting Bull had slashed his arms one hundred times and then danced for eighteen hours while offering prayers to the great spirit *Wakan Tanka*. After collapsing in exhaustion, Sitting Bull reportedly had a vision in which hundreds of soldiers fell into his camp and died. Believing that the vision signified a great victory, he told his people, "These dead soldiers are the gifts of [the great spirit]." A day after Custer passed the site, Sitting Bull's vision would become reality in the Battle of the Little Bighorn.

Custer with his Arikara scouts in 1874, when his troops were guarding railroad crews building the Northern Pacific Railroad in Montana. Bloody Knife, front left, one of Custer's favorite scouts, was killed at the Little Bighorn. Other army scouts on the Plains were Crow. Both the Crow and Arikara peoples were traditional enemies of the Sioux, who had taken over their ancestral homelands on the Plains.

through the day of the battle, including some 20 miles (32 km) the day of the fight. On the night of June 24, Crow scouts told Custer the Native camp was at the Little Bighorn. Worried that the people might flee before he could attack, Custer ordered a night march to the Native camp.

Custer's men set out about midnight, traveling 6 miles (10 km) in two hours before stopping to sleep just short of the Crow's Nest, a tall hill overlooking the Little Bighorn which was some 15 miles (24 km) distant. At dawn, Custer climbed the hill. Even though he could not see it well, he knew the village was far bigger than expected. It was then Custer made the most fateful decision of his life. He told his troops, "The largest Indian camp on the North American continent is ahead and I'm going to attack it."

27

# The Battle of the Little Bighorn

This pictograph by Red Horse, a Sioux warrior who fought at the Little Bighorn, shows Custer's troops approaching the village.

On the morning of June 25, 1876, when Custer stood on the Crow's Nest, he could only dimly see the camp 15 miles (24 km) away. Earlier reports had indicated Custer would encounter a village of about 3,000, which would mean a fighting force of about 800 warriors. But in the week before the battle, the encampment more than doubled with the arrival of reservation Indians. It had swollen to nearly 7,000 Sioux, Cheyenne, and Arapaho men, women, and children. There were an estimated 2,000 warriors.

Custer's scouts warned their chief that it would be dangerous to attack such a large camp, but he ignored them. Confident in his leadership and his men, Custer boasted that day, "I could whip all the Indians on the continent with the Seventh Cavalry." Some historians also believe he was relying on what was known as "Custer's luck," his unfailing ability to win big battles and remain unharmed. But Custer's luck was about to desert him.

## Custer's Plan

Custer and his men continued on and halted southeast of the Native village at the head of what would later be named Reno Creek. Low hills hid them from the camp, but Custer, fearing the Indians would flee if they spotted his troops, decided to split his force into three units. His plan was patterned after Sheridan's original strategy to trap the Indians.

Shortly after noon, Custer ordered Major Marcus Reno and 140 men to

Major Marcus Reno commanded three companies at the Battle of the Little Bighorn. His troops attacked the Native village by the river and then retreated in panic and confusion onto what is now called Reno Hill, where they stayed until the battle was over. Reno was later accused of cowardice.

## George Armstrong Custer (1839—1876)

Born in New Rumley, Ohio, George Armstrong Custer graduated in 1862 from West Point, the U.S. military academy. Although Custer finished last in his class, he became a hero in the Civil War in battles such as Bull Run and Gettysburg. Promoted to brigadier general at the age of only twenty-three, he was the youngest to ever hold that rank. Custer became known as the "boy general." After the Civil War ended, his rank was reduced to captain, but in 1866 he became a lieutenant colonel when the Seventh Cavalry was formed. Custer's reputation grew with his victories against Native Americans. He was a daring and resourceful officer, but Custer was also vain, and many consider him a "glory hound" because he sought fame so fiercely. After his death, he achieved what he had hoped for when the story of the Battle of the Little Bighorn spread around the world.

## The Coming of Long Hair

"I was hostile to the white man . . . we preferred hunting to a life of idleness on our reservations. At times we did not get enough to eat and we were not allowed to hunt. All we wanted was peace and to be left alone. Soldiers came and destroyed our villages. Then Long Hair [Custer] came. They say we massacred him, but he would have done the same to us. Our first impulse was to escape but we were so hemmed in we had to fight."

*Oglala war chief Crazy Horse*

proceed along the left bank of Reno Creek, cross the Little Bighorn, and attack the village's south end. To seal off escape routes in the valley, he sent Captain Frederick Benteen and 125 soldiers to the south. Custer kept about 225 men, half under the command of Captain George Yates and half led by Captain Myles Keogh. Custer then followed Reno Creek on the right side, parallel to Benteen. The **pack train** with extra ammunition and supplies brought up the rear.

## Reno's Charge

About 2:00 P.M., Custer and Reno's units met 4 miles (6 km) from the village.

After crossing the Little Bighorn where it meets Reno Creek, Reno's men retreated to Reno Hill, shown here. This map also shows Battle Ridge and Custer Hill, where Custer's men were surrounded by warriors led by Crazy Horse and Gall.

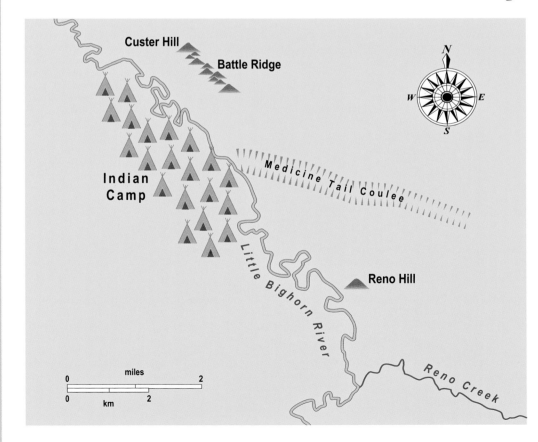

30

When scouts spotted people fleeing toward the river, Custer wanted an immediate attack. In a written message, he ordered Reno to "move at as rapid a gait as you think prudent and to charge [the Indian village] afterwards, and you will be supported by this whole outfit."

When Reno's unit attacked at 3:00 P.M., a wave of mounted warriors came streaming out of the village. Reno's men dismounted and began firing into the village, which was several hundred yards away. The people had known soldiers were in the area, but Oglala Chief Low Dog later said, "I did not think it possible that any white man would attack us, so strong as we were. . . . I lost no time in getting ready."

Neither did hundreds of warriors who engaged Reno in battle. Overwhelmed within a few minutes, Reno retreated. In his official report, Reno painted a terrifying description of his situation: "The very earth seemed to grow Indians, and they were running toward me in swarms, and from all directions. I saw I must defend myself and give up the attack." Reno retreated along the Little Bighorn into the woods, then crossed the river and took a stronger defensive position in high **bluffs**. By this time, forty of Reno's men had been killed and thirteen wounded.

When Benteen rode up shortly after 4:00 P.M., Reno pleaded with him to stay: "For God's sake, halt your command and help me!" Benteen, Reno, and the pack train, which soon came up, joined forces on what became known as Reno Hill.

## Custer Advances
After splitting from Reno, Custer's troops headed north of the encampment. When Custer saw the strong **counterattack** against

Captain Frederick Benteen, like Reno, was accused of failing to do his duty at the Little Bighorn. He was slow to respond to Custer's desperate summons.

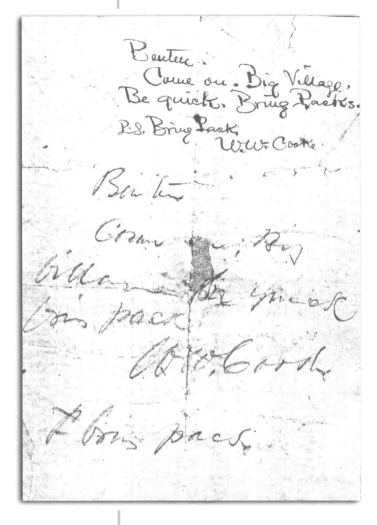

This is the note dictated by Custer that Cooke sent to Benteen. The scrawled words and repetition indicate the desperation with which it was written. The message has been written out more clearly at the top by Benteen.

Reno, he realized he faced a tougher fight than expected. He sent Sergeant Daniel Kanipe back to the pack train with a message that included the phrase, "Come quick. Big Indian camp."

Custer continued north to Medicine Tail **Coulee**. Anxious for support from Benteen, Custer ordered trumpeter John Martin to carry a message written by staff officer William W. Cooke: "Benteen. Come on. Big Village. Be quick. Bring packs. W. W. Cooke. P. S. Bring packs." This was the last message from Custer, who then split up his forces once again in his plan to charge the village. About 4:00 P.M., Custer ordered Yates to descend Medicine Tail Coulee to the Little Bighorn River while he sent Keogh's men up Medicine Tail's north slope. Within a short time, both units would be attacked.

## At The River

Precisely what happened in this famous battle will never be known. Many of the eyewitness accounts of the fight are thought to be unreliable, and they do indeed contain many conflicting facts. By sifting through the personal accounts of Native warriors and U.S. soldiers and studying the battlefield itself, however, historians have pieced together some details.

When Yates took his men down to the Little Bighorn, warriors concealed in brush on the other side of the river began firing on the soldiers. Sitting Bull, who did not fight himself, described the encounter this way: "Our young men rained lead across the river and drove the white **braves** back."

At first, only a handful of warriors held Yates in check. But then Gall, a Hunkpapa Sioux famed for his bravery, rallied maybe as many as fifteen hundred warriors. They crossed the river and forced the soldiers to retreat to the bluffs behind them.

This drawing of the battle is by Oglala Sioux Amos Bad Heart Bull. He shows Crazy Horse in the center wearing spotted war paint.

## Crazy Horse Strikes

Next to Sitting Bull, the most famous Sioux at the Little Bighorn was Oglala war chief Crazy Horse, a master strategist. While Gall

## Crazy Horse (c. 1840—1877)

Crazy Horse, or Tasunke Witko, was an Oglala Sioux, a great warrior, and a brilliant leader. He was also a very thoughtful person who carefully considered his actions. He led the Sioux in the Fetterman incident in 1866, and at the time of the Little Bighorn battle, Crazy Horse was war chief of the Sioux nation.

Crazy Horse was a warrior who loved his people. When someone once asked him where his lands were, Crazy Horse answered: "My lands are where my dead lie buried." Crazy Horse surrendered to the U.S. Army in May 1877 and died after being stabbed by a soldier later that year. No accurate image of Crazy Horse is known to exist as he never allowed himself to be photographed or painted.

This painting by W. H. Dunton shows the traditional view of Custer's Last Stand with Custer's men on the ridge surrounded by Sioux and Cheyenne warriors.

led his forces after Custer's unit, Crazy Horse rallied other warriors in the village by shouting a traditional battle chant. According to witnesses, he called "Ho-ka hey! It is a good day to fight! It is a good day to die! Strong hearts, brave hearts, to the front! Weak hearts and cowards to the rear."

Meanwhile, Custer's men had sought higher ground to make a defensive stand and had ended up on what became known as Battle Ridge. When Crazy Horse led hundreds of warriors out of the village, they also headed up to Battle Ridge. It may be that Crazy Horse had quickly devised a plan to strike Custer's units from a different direction. Or he may have been getting ready to defend the fleeing villagers from another attack.

When Crazy Horse streamed over the top, he caught Custer's men between his warriors and those of Gall. The combined forces overwhelmed the outnumbered white soldiers.

The final attempt by soldiers to save themselves is famed as Custer's Last Stand. This took place on what is now known as Custer Hill, on the western slope of the northern end of Battle Ridge. It was here that about forty soldiers shot their horses so they could shelter behind them to fight. There is evidence to show that other men ran down into Deep Ravine, below the ridge, and that they may have been the last to die. Within a short time, all the soldiers had been killed. Cheyenne Chief Two Moons claimed, "It took about as long as it takes a hungry man to eat his lunch."

## Where Did Custer Die?

Historians, however, are not sure if Custer actually died at the Last Stand. Although his body was found on Custer Hill, some eyewitness accounts claim he was killed at the river. His men could have moved Custer to the hill to protect his body.

### Two Moons' Story

"The shooting was quick. Pop-pop-pop very fast. Some of the soldiers were down on their knees, some standing. The smoke was like a great cloud, and everywhere the Sioux went the dust rose like smoke. We circled all round [the soldiers] swirling like water round a stone. We shoot, we ride fast, we shoot again. Soldiers drop and horses fall on them. Indians keep swirling round and round, and the soldiers killed only a few. Many soldiers fell. At last all horses killed but five. Once in a while some man would break out and run towards the river, but he would fall. At last about a hundred men stood on the hill all bunched together. All along the bugler kept blowing his commands. He was very brave too. Then a chief was killed. I hear it was Long Hair [Custer], I don't know. All the soldiers were now killed, and the bodies were stripped. After that no one could tell which were officers."

*Cheyenne Chief Two Moons describing his view of the Battle of the Little Bighorn*

Custer and other members of the Seventh Cavalry took a camping trip some weeks before the battle. Several of the men shown here died at the Little Bighorn. Custer is standing in the center in his fringed jacket.

The night of June 25, 1876, soldiers remained on Reno Hill (in the foreground above) looking down on the Little Bighorn River below. They heard the sound of drums and chants coming from the village and saw the glow of huge fires by the river.

In an interview with a *New York Herald* reporter a year after the Battle of the Little Bighorn, Sitting Bull helped foster this most lasting image of the battle—Custer fighting to the death on the hill: "It was said that up there where the last fight took place, where the last stand took place, the Long Hair [Custer's Indian nickname] stood like a sheaf of corn with all the ears [bodies of his soldiers] fallen around him. His hair was as the color of the grass when the frost comes."

Sitting Bull claims Custer was killed after shooting a warrior with a pistol. But because the chief did not witness the battle, the accuracy of his account has been questioned.

George was not the only Custer who died that day. With him were his brothers Thomas, a captain who had twice received the Medal of Honor, and Boston, a civilian guide. Others in his family who died were Harry Reed (a nephew who came to see the expected battle) and Custer's brother-in-law James Calhoun.

## The Rest of the Battle

The fighting at Battle Ridge was over quickly, but not the whole battle. The warriors now attacked Benteen and Reno, who had formed a defensive perimeter on Reno Hill. The soldiers stopped the initial charge, but the two sides fought until 9:00 P.M., when the warriors ceased firing. They went back to their village, where they danced and feasted after their great victory.

The Plains warriors resumed their attack the next day, June 26, but the U.S. soldiers had dug into the earth and improved their defenses. The warriors circled closer and kept firing all day, but they did not charge. By late afternoon, only an occasional shot came from the Indian side. That night, the village broke up, and the groups that had gathered there moved away. The battle was finally over.

On the morning of June 27, 1876, General Terry and Colonel Gibbon arrived at the site. It was Lieutenant J. H. Bradley, Gibbon's chief of scouts, who discovered Custer and his slain men. Of Custer, Bradley later wrote: "His expression was rather that of a man who has fallen asleep and enjoyed peaceful dreams than that of one who met his death amid such fearful scenes as that field had witnessed." Like his men's, Custer's body had been stripped of its clothes and weapons.

This photograph, taken between 1877 and 1879, shows the battlefield at the Little Bighorn after the battle. Horse bones and soldiers' boots were still scattered on the hillside, and wooden markers showed where soldiers had died.

# After the Battle

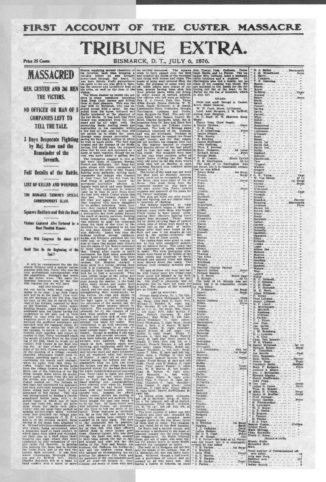

A newspaper announces the Battle of the Little Bighorn to Americans on July 6, 1876.

## White Revenge

The first stories about the battle did not appear in newspapers until several days after the United States had celebrated the hundredth birthday of its independence. "The Red Man's Revenge" was the shocking headline in the *Atlanta Constitution* on July 7. The *Chicago Tribune* proclaimed, "A Feeling of the Most Bitter Resentment Awakened in the Country." The latter headline summed up the mood of an entire nation. Americans wanted to punish all Native people for the deaths of Custer and his men.

Thousands of soldiers pursued the Plains people who had dispersed into their own groups after the battle. Within a few months, the army had defeated most of them and forced them back onto reservations. In July 1876, the reservations were put under military control. The United States took possession of the Black Hills and Powder River region and moved many Sioux to reservations on the Missouri River. On February 28, 1877, Congress passed a law that officially ended Sioux ownership of the Black Hills.

## The Custer Myth

Countless books have been written about Custer, and hundreds of paintings have tried to portray his epic Last Stand. By dying at the Little Bighorn, Custer achieved the historical immortality he had always desired. From the first news of his death, many Americans have revered Custer as a hero. This has occurred even though many people believed he was foolish to challenge such a large Native force and that he made poor decisions during the battle. President

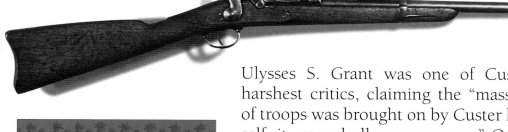

Ulysses S. Grant was one of Custer's harshest critics, claiming the "massacre of troops was brought on by Custer himself, it was wholly unnecessary." Others blamed Major Reno and Captain Benteen for failing to help Custer when he was attacked.

## Sitting Bull, Crazy Horse

Sitting Bull and Crazy Horse did not have long to celebrate their victory. After being pursued constantly by the army, Crazy Horse surrendered May 6, 1877, at Fort Robinson in Nebraska. On September 6, 1877, when he returned to Fort Robinson to meet with officials, soldiers arrested him. While his arms were held, a soldier stabbed him to death with a bayonet.

For years after the battle, weapons and other relics of the battle were found at the Little Bighorn. This rifle from the battlefield is a Springfield carbine made in 1873 for the U.S. Cavalry.

### Everlasting Fame

"In years long numbered with the past, when I was verging upon manhood, my every thought was ambitious—not to be wealthy, not to be learned, but to be great. I desired to link my name with a mark of honor—not only to the present, but to future generations."

*George Armstrong Custer*

## The End of Resistance

One result of Little Bighorn was that the United States Army began to deal more harshly with other tribes such as the Nez Percé of Idaho, Washington, and Oregon and the Apaches of the Southwest. After a brief war caused by the government's demand that the Nez Percé leave their traditional home, Nez Percé leader Chief Joseph surrendered on October 5, 1877, declaring, "I will fight no more forever." His statement was true by then of almost all Native Americans. When the fierce Apache war chief Geronimo ceased fighting on September 4, 1886, organized Native resistance to white settlement finally ended.

The U.S. Army gathers up bodies of the Miniconjou people slain at Wounded Knee. The massacre on the Pine Ridge reservation in 1890 was a final defeat for the Plains people.

In May 1877, Sitting Bull and some four hundred Hunkpapa Sioux fled to Canada, where they hoped to live peacefully. But life was harsh, and Sitting Bull eventually surrendered so his people could be taken care of on a reservation. On July 19, 1881, Sitting Bull gave himself up at Fort Buford in the Dakota Territory, saying, "Let it be recorded that I am the last man of my people to lay down my gun."

In 1886, Sitting Bull again became a celebrity when he toured with Buffalo Bill's "Wild West" show. He remained an influential Sioux leader until his death in December 1890. Reservation officials wanted Sitting Bull arrested, fearing he would lead a new Sioux uprising, and he was shot and killed by reservation policemen during the course of his arrest.

## Wounded Knee

The death of Sitting Bull led to the last great tragedy in the long war between the Sioux and whites. This took place on December 29, 1890, at Wounded Knee, a creek on the Pine Ridge Indian reservation in southwestern South Dakota. The victims were members of a group of more than three hundred Miniconjou people led by Hunkpapa Chief Big Foot. Fearing reprisals after Sitting Bull's death, they had left the reservation to camp on the Cheyenne River. The Seventh Cavalry had forced them back to Wounded Knee. Big Foot had already surrendered, but a fight broke out when the U.S. Army demanded the Miniconjous' weapons. The outnumbered Miniconjous were gunned down with **Hotchkiss guns**.

The Army suffered about twenty-five casualties, but more than two hundred Sioux men, women, and children were slain by the Seventh Cavalry. Many historians believe Wounded Knee was a final stroke of vengeance for the death of Custer and his men at the Battle of the Little Bighorn. A mass grave was dug, and the bodies were thrown in. A civilian who helped bury the victims was horrified: "It is a thing to melt the heart of a man, if it was of stone, to see those little children, with their bodies shot to pieces thrown naked into the [burial] pit."

This 1891 photograph by John Grabill is entitled "The Great Hostile Indian Camp." It shows a gathering of Sioux near Pine Ridge in South Dakota. These people had left their reservation cabins in a last gesture of freedom.

# Conclusion

The Little Bighorn River still flows clear and cold. The lush, gently rolling hills surrounding it are still covered with the greasy grass that fed buffalo and enabled the people of the Plains to live their traditional lives.

Visitors to the Little Bighorn battlefield can walk the hills where the fighting took place. All over the battlefield are white markers, like gravestones, at the spots where the bodies of U.S. soldiers were found.

### Common Goals

"All Americans—Indians and non-Indians—should continue to remember the events of June 25, 1876, but seek to narrow the differences which keep us from achieving our common goals."

*U.S. Senator Ben Nighthorse, speaking at the 125th anniversary of the Little Bighorn in 2001*

## A National Monument

At first, the battlefield site was designated a burial ground for Seventh Cavalry soldiers who died in that fierce struggle and other members of the U.S. Army who served in the West. In 1940, the National Park Service began caring for the cemetery, and it was named Custer Battlefield National Monument. It had become an increasingly popular destination for people interested in its history.

In 1992, the site was re-christened as the Little Bighorn Battlefield National Monument to reflect also the Native side of this famous battle. Lying in the heart of the Crow Indian reservation of southeastern Montana, the battlefield is visited by some 400,000 people every year. A monument to slain soldiers stands in the burial ground at Little Bighorn, and a museum at the visitor center teaches visitors about the site and the battle.

## No Native Memorial

Estimates of Native American fatalities in the battle range from thirty to three hundred, but there is no memorial at

In the Black Hills, an image of Crazy Horse is being carved out of a mountain. Started in 1948, it will be the world's biggest sculpture when it is finished. The model in the foreground shows what the sculpture will look like when it is completed.

the site to honor the Plains Indians. In 1988, the American Indian Movement placed a plaque at the foot of the monument honoring slain soldiers. The plaque read, "In Honor of our Indian patriots who fought and defeated the U.S. Cavalry in order to save our women and children from mass murder." Officials took the plaque down, but it is on display in the museum. In 1991, Congress authorized a Native memorial, but only if it was paid for by private funds. To date, not enough money has been raised to build it.

## Legacy of the Little Bighorn

The legacy of the victory in the Battle of the Little Bighorn has been a sad one. The Plains people were soon defeated in other battles, and the federal government forced them to live on reservations that made up only a tiny fraction of the millions of acres of land they once roamed. Today, descendants of the people at the Little Bighorn live in poverty on reservations such as Pine Ridge, home to more than 38,000 Lakota Sioux. Pine Ridge includes the nation's two poorest counties. There, the Sioux struggle to become educated and find jobs. During periods in the 1990s, unemployment stood at 80 percent. The community suffers from many health problems, including alcoholism, which affects eight out of ten families.

# Time Line

1864    ■   November 29: Sand Creek Massacre in Colorado.

1866    ■   U.S. Army begins building three forts along the Bozeman Trail to protect travelers.
December 21: Fetterman Massacre.

1868    ■   November 9: Sioux and Cheyenne agree to the Treaty of Fort Laramie, ending Red Cloud's War.
November 27: Battle of the Washita in Oklahoma.

1874    ■   July 2–August 30: Lt. Col. George Armstrong Custer leads an expedition that discovers gold in the Black Hills.

1875    ■   December: U.S. government orders all Sioux to report to reservations by January 31, 1876.

1876    ■   February: U.S. Army begins planning how to round up "hostile" Indians.
May 17: Custer leaves Fort Abraham Lincoln with General Alfred Terry.
June 17: Sioux and Cheyenne attack General George Crook's troops at Rosebud Creek.
June 22: Custer's unit moves toward the Little Bighorn River.
June 25: Battle of the Little Bighorn.
June 26: Plains people abandon siege at Reno Hill.
June 27: General Terry and Colonel John Gibbon arrive at the Little Bighorn battle site.

1877    ■   February 28 : Act of Congress takes the Black Hills and ends all Sioux rights outside the Great Sioux Reservation.
September 6: Crazy Horse is killed at Fort Robinson.
October 5: Nez Percé Chief Joseph surrenders.

1886    ■   September 4: Apache Chief Geronimo surrenders.

1890    ■   December 15: Sitting Bull is killed by Indian police.
December 29: Massacre at Wounded Knee.

1940    ■   Little Bighorn battlefield is named Custer Battlefield National Monument.

1948    ■   Crazy Horse sculpture is started in Black Hills.

1992    ■   Custer Battlefield National Monument is renamed Little Bighorn Battlefield National Monument.

# Glossary

**bluff:** steep bank or cliff above a river, lake, or coastline.

**brave:** Native American warrior.

**breech-loading:** describes a gun loaded with cartridges, enabling it to fire much faster than one that is muzzle-loaded.

**cavalry:** soldiers who travel and fight on horseback.

**column:** line of soldiers.

**coulee:** small stream or streambed and the small ravine between two hills containing such a streambed.

**counterattack:** return attack after being attacked.

**emigrant:** person who leaves his or her place of residence to go and live somewhere else.

**federal:** to do with national government.

**hardtack:** type of hard bread or biscuit.

**Hotchkiss gun:** early machine gun made in France.

**infantry:** soldiers who travel and fight on foot.

**manifest:** obviously true and easily recognizable. When white Americans used the phrase "Manifest Destiny," they meant it was obviously their destiny to take over the North American continent.

**muzzle-loader:** firearm loaded by pouring gunpowder down the barrel.

**nation:** group of Native American people. The term is used to mean large groups including many tribes but can also refer to a tribe or a confederation of tribes.

**natural resources:** naturally occurring materials, such as wood, oil, and gold, that can be used or sold.

**nomadic:** traveling around as a way of life rather than living in one place.

**pack train:** string of horses or mules used to carry packs (bundles of supplies).

**prospector:** person who explores an area looking for mineral resources such as gold or oil.

**regular:** enlisted soldier in the official army of a nation.

**reservation:** public land set aside for Native American people to live on when they were removed from their homelands.

**scout:** member of a group or army sent in advance to find information, such as the whereabouts of an enemy.

**trapper:** hunter who uses traps to kill animals such as beaver or squirrel for their fur.

**treaty:** agreement made between two or more people or groups of people after negotiation, often at the end of a period of conflict.

**unceded:** not granted or given to anyone.

# Further Information

## Books

Cunningham, Chet. *Crazy Horse: War Chief of the Oglalas.* Lerner Publications, 2000.

Krehbiel, Randy. *Little Bighorn.* Twenty-First Century Books, 1997.

Marcovitz, Hal. *George Custer* (*Famous Figures of the American Frontier* series). Chelsea House, 2001.

Sita, Lisa. *Indians of the Great Plains: Traditions, History, Legends, and Life.* Gareth Stevens, 2000.

Viola, Herman J., ed. *It Is a Good Day to Die: Indian Eyewitnesses Tell the Story of the Battle of the Little Bighorn.* Bison Books, 2001.

## Web Sites

**www.crazyhorse.org** Dedicated to the Crazy Horse Memorial, the huge statue being carved out of a mountain in the Black Hills.

**www.mohicanpress.com/battles/ba04002.html** Photographs of various sites at the Little Bighorn battlefield.

**www.nps.gov/libi** Maintained by the National Park Service of the Department of the Interior, with interesting information about the Little Bighorn Battlefield National Monument and maps and pictures of the battle.

## Useful Addresses

**Little Bighorn Battlefield National Monument**
National Park Service
P. O. Box 39
Crow Agency, MT 59022
Telephone: (406) 638-2621

# Index

Page numbers in *italics* indicate maps and diagrams. Page numbers in **bold** indicate other illustrations.